The Pirate's Journal

A Modern Treasure Hunters Guide to Wealth Building

- Charissa Turnbull -

in omnia paratus publishing

www.inomniaparatuspublishing.com

TABLE OF CONTENTS

Pirate Principle One:
The Most Valuable Treasure and a Ship to Seek It.................................. 5

Pirate Principle Two
Set your Compass Due North.................................. 17

Pirate Principle Three
Using Blackbeard's Spyglass.................................. 25

Pirate Principle Four
Make Shame and Guilt Walk the Plank.................................. 33

Pirate Principle Five
Build a Treasure Chest for Your Gold.................................. 45

Pirate Principle Six
The Pirate's Life is the Life for Me.................................. 49

Pirate Principle Seven
How to Split the Booty.................................. 53

Pirate Principle Eight
The Obligations of a Pirate Cartographer.................................. 59

Template Library.................................. 67

Reflection Pages 75

"Money is only a tool. It will take you wherever you wish, but it will not replace you as the driver."

– Ayn Rand

PIRATE PRINCIPLE ONE

PIRATE PRINCIPLE ONE

The Most Valuable Treasure and a Ship to Seek It

It is no secret that in pirate times and even in modern times, a map (or GPS) in our case, is key to getting to places we have never been and discovering uncharted territories.

Think of the explorers that risked their lives to map out new lands, the sailors that dedicated their lives to sailing the seas and discovering uncharted territories. Society would not be what it is today without these adventure seekers.

So, what does this have to do with money and you?

Simple really, when you learn to create maps for yourself from a place of exploration and discovery, wealth building happens with ease!

We will be creating several maps in this program but the first one is the most important, we are going to discover what makes us FEEL financially secure and create it.

In *"The Broken Ladder"* by Keith Payne he talks about how feelings of being broke have the same psychological impact as actually being broke. So if you FEEL broke you make decisions as if you are broke. If you FEEL secure you make decisions from that place.

We will go much deeper into this concept as we move through this course but for now I want to talk about the opposite of this... why this is important even if you FEEL like you are abundant, spend money with ease because it is always there...

I tell people all the time, I was better with money when I was poor and that is true. I spent less frivolously but I was MUCH worse at wealth building because I was afraid of needing it later. As we made more money, we had too big of an emergency fund, were way to hung up on being debt free and were not open to opportunity - right up until we were!

Risk is what creates wealth and if you don't think you are in this place of lack because you have plenty, ask yourself how risk averse are you?

JOURNAL PROMPT

Use the reflection pages provided to answer journal prompts! There are additional blank pages at the back of this workbook.

How much do you make in your busiest 3 month period?

If you are on a salary, think of bonus time. The idea is that this should be the most money you have ever made in a 90 day period.

Now think of your slowest time of the year. Same as above, has there been a 90 day period where you have made significantly less than the first answer? If not use the same number, it will still work.

The Most Money I've made in 90 Days:

_____

The Least Money I've made in 90 Days:

_____

Now I want you to imagine that you have to take 100% of the first amount and spend it on an investment. It cannot stay in savings. It cannot go in a CD, Money Market or anything not projected to make you at least 20%...

Think High Risk Investment....

Describe in detail how this makes you feel?

Really imagine yourself "risking" this money.

How will this impact the leaner times?

Remember you are investing 100%, not 100% after your bills are paid...

Ahoy! AVAST means STOP in pirate lingo! Every time you see this symbol, go to the reflection pages at the back of this book to take action and journal your thoughts!

JOURNAL PROMPT

Use the reflection pages provided to answer journal prompts! There are additional blank pages at the back of this workbook.

Picture this...

(I heard this one from my coach and it is too good not to share!)

Let's say I had a beach house in Maui worth $5 million.

I offer to sell it to you for that first number. The number you just imagined investing...

How do you feel about investing 100% of that money now?

Other Questions to Consider

On a scale of 1-10 how risk averse do you think you are?

Are you happy with this number?

Do you think this holds you back in any way?

STOP! Go to the reflection pages at the back of this book to take action and journal your thoughts!

Creating Your Map to Financial Stability

Imagining Financial Freedom.

Picture this: You never have to work a day in your life again if you don't want to. You do whatever you want when you want to do it. You invest freely as you see opportunities. You will never say no because of money ever again.

Step 1 - Describe in detail the following:

1. How much money do you make?

2. How many sources of income do you have? What are they and how much does each bring in?

3. How much do you donate to charity - remember this your ideal scenario

4. How much money is in your checking account, savings accounts, what other accounts do you have and how much is in each?

5. How do you spend that money? How many vacations do you go on, what kind of house do you live in, what kind of car do you drive…

STOP! Go to the reflection pages at the back of this book to take action and journal your thoughts!

As you do the exercise...

Really lean into that feeling of financial freedom. Really see yourself in these situations. Imagine your partner there with you, what do they drive, how does this impact their lives…

Step 2 – Think of your life now and write about the differences:

Focus on how you feel about the differences.

Go back and read your answer to step 1 again. If you could only pick 1 of those things, what would it be?

Example:

For me, it is multiple sources of income, it could be liquid savings,, for some it is contributions to 401K, sometimes it is a college fund. It doesn't matter which one it is, but you can only pick one.

STOP! Go to the reflection pages at the back of this book to take action and journal your thoughts!

Step 3 – Why did you pick that thing?

How does it make you feel? What does having that thing represent to you?

Go deep here, the deeper you go the better your map will be.

STOP! Go to the reflection pages at the back of this book to take action and journal your thoughts!

Step 4 - Write out 25 Money Beliefs:

Write out a minimum 25 beliefs you believe or that you have been told about money. This could be from parents, grandparents, bosses, mentors, society as a whole. Write down everything you can think of.

When you are done, go through and rank them 1, 2 or 3.
1 = Things you believe
2 = Things you sort of / maybe believe
3 = Things you do not believe

Money Belief	Rank: 1	2	3
1.			
2.			
3.			
4.			
5.			
6.			
7.			
8.			
9.			
10.			
11.			
12.			
13.			
14.			
15.			
16.			
17.			
18.			
19.			
20.			
21.			
22.			
23.			
24.			
25.			

Step 5: Make a new list with Just 1's and 2's:

As you look at each one ask yourself. "Does this belief help me reach my goals or not?" (It does not matter how much you believe it to be true, answer the question honestly) Each entry should have a yes or a no.

Go back through the same list and ask yourself "Is this a belief I WANT to keep or not? Circle everything you're keeping.

Need more room to write? -- Use the reflection pages at the back of this book!

Money Belief

	Yes	No
1.	☐	☐
2.	☐	☐
3.	☐	☐
4.	☐	☐
5.	☐	☐
6.	☐	☐
7.	☐	☐
8.	☐	☐
9.	☐	☐
10.	☐	☐
11.	☐	☐
12.	☐	☐
13.	☐	☐
14.	☐	☐
15.	☐	☐
16.	☐	☐
17.	☐	☐
18.	☐	☐
19.	☐	☐
20.	☐	☐
21.	☐	☐
22.	☐	☐
23.	☐	☐
24.	☐	☐
25.	☐	☐

Step 6: Time to Make that map!

Now comes the fun part! You get to take all of the things we have just done and identify the 6 steps that will get you from where you are now to feeling fully financially stable! Think of this as what you would need to have in place to do all the things in the very first journal exercise without stress, fear, or guilt!

These steps may have smaller steps under them so these should be you 6 big picture steps. They are like landmarks on a map! This could include letting go of some of those money beliefs in step 4 and 5, it could include things to more fully live the ones you want to keep. The thing is you, only get 6 steps so make them count! At the end of the 6 steps you need to have landed on X!

If you are having a hard time with this, go back and read the journal entries you have made while really thinking about 'What is holding me back from having this?"

STOP! Make sure to complete this activity on the next 2 pages before moving on in the workbook! If you need more space – use the reflection pages in the back of this workbook.

THE TREASURE TRAIL TO YOUR DREAM LIFE

Describe your current feelings about money in 2 sentences or less.

START

Landmark #1:

Landmark #2:

Landmark #3:

Landmark #4:

Landmark #5:

Landmark #6:

X MARKS THE SPOT

Your X is the 1 thing you picked from your dream life!

CREATING YOUR PIRATE SHIP

(Psst. You Already Have It!)

The Truth is, the object you need to seek your treasure and follow your map is right here in your hand. We will be building it as we go. It is this journal and the person you are becoming as you use it!

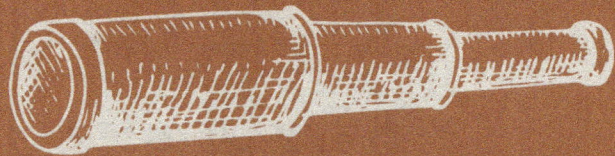

ACTIVITY PROMPT

Time for Accountability!

1. Take a picture of your completed treasure map and post it in the group!

2. What 3 things are you committed to this week to help you reach your first landmark? Post it in the group!

AVAST

STOP! Have you completed all the action steps in this section? Double check before continuing...

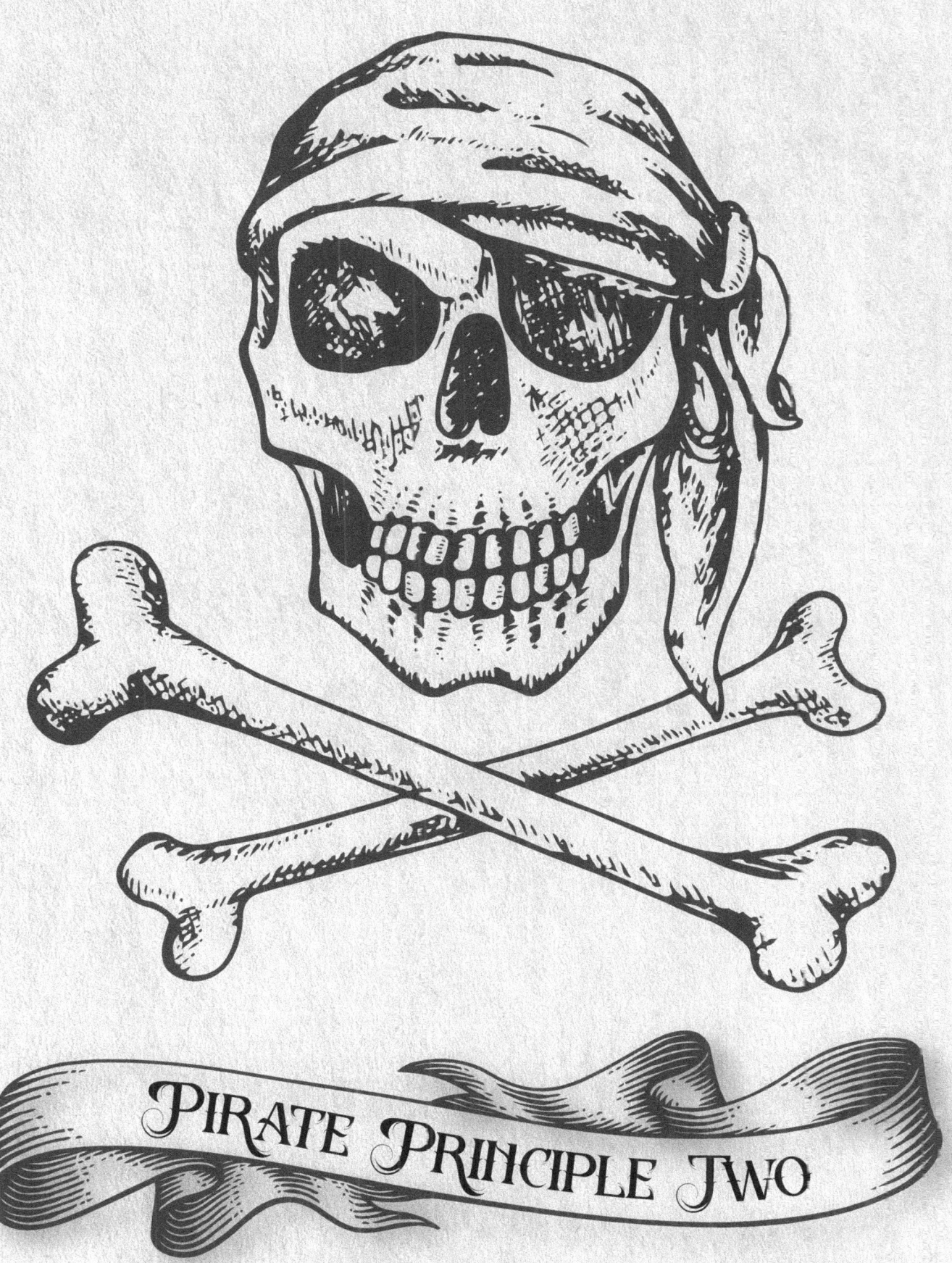

PIRATE PRINCIPLE TWO

PIRATE PRINCIPLE TWO

Set your Compass Due North!

Now that you have created your first map, it is time to make it even better! As we go through this course, you will be building a map that relates to each pirate principle. At the end, each one of these maps will represent a Major landmark on your larger map to prosperity isle and will give you everything you need to create alignment in your wealth building strategies!

For the 2nd map, we will be mapping to that Dream Life you created in Part 1 of the last module!

Take a moment and go back and read what you wrote.

Step 1 - Focus on the Detail

Write it out again, but this time, in even more detail!

Don't forget to include HOW YOU FEEL in each area of life! Here is a hint, the chart below shows the 8 main areas of life we are shooting to have alignment in!

As you describe your life, try and get as many of these in the description as possible!

Where are you living, not just the house but the location, neighborhood? What kind of yard do you have? What are the neighbors like? What do you do in your spare time? Who is with you? Are you married? Do you have kids? Pets? Do you travel all the time and live a nomadic life?

AVAST *STOP! Go to the reflection pages at the back of this book to take action and journal your thoughts!*

Health

Environment

Wealth

Time

AREAS OF FOCUS

Self

Career

Relationships

Personal Development

Step 2 - Analyze the differences:

Just like step 2 of the first Pirate Principle, we are going to analyze the differences. While you go through them, this time I want you to really think about why you do not have this life yet.

This is absolutely NOT an invitation to kick your own ass! When I say think about the why, I mean think about timing, relationships you don't have yet, skills you will need to master to get there, opportunities that have not presented themselves yet!

You can include changes you want to make right now of course but make sure you include both! If you do choose to look at changes you want to make, ask yourself why. Not just why you want to change but why you made those past choices. It is important to honor the person that got us to where we are, even as we look to improve ourselves and circumstances!

STOP! Go to the reflection pages at the back of this book to take action and journal your thoughts!

Step 3 - Brain Dump:

Time for a good old fashioned brain dump exercise!!! Take 3 deep breaths and really see that life you want, feel it, where is it in your body, what does it remind you of, what color is it?

Now, Set the timer for 5 minutes and write all the ways you could get that life. Realistic is not in your vocabulary today! Winning the lottery is a completely viable answer. Write for the full 5 minutes, every single thing that comes to mind gets written down, it is important not to filter yourself!

Look at your list, is there anything on it that if it happened you would immediately have your dream life? Exaple: Lottery - Money to do whatever I want.

STOP! Go to the reflection pages at the back of this book to take action and journal your thoughts!

Step 4 - Refine:

Go through your list and really think about how those things get you to your dream life in all 8 areas. Anything that can cover 3 or more areas, circle it.

What is the thing about the circled ideas that makes them work? Why do these things move you forward in more than one area?

Now answer the following question:

What 6 things do I need to achieve my dream life in all 8 areas? You only get 6 so make them count!

STOP! Go to the reflection pages at the back of this book to take action and journal your thoughts!

Step 5 - Plug them into a map:

Describe your current life in a few sentences. This should be a summary of where you are in the 8 areas. Once again - not an excuse to kick your own ass! If it makes it easier, rank yourself 1-10 in each category and start there!

Landmark 1
Landmark 2
Landmark 3
Landmark 4
Landmark 5
Landmark 6

X marks the spot!

Your X is your dream life

STOP! Make sure to complete this activity on the next 2 pages before moving on in the workbook! If you need more space - use the reflection pages in the back of this workbook.

THE DREAM LIFE TREASURE TRAIL CONTINUES

Describe your current life in a few sentences. This should be a summary of where you are in the 8 areas.

START

_____
_____
_____
_____

Landmark #1:

_____
_____
_____
_____
_____
_____

Landmark #2:

_____
_____
_____
_____
_____

Landmark #3:

_____
_____
_____
_____
_____

Landmark #4:

Landmark #5:

Landmark #6:

X MARKS THE SPOT

Your X is the 1 thing you picked from your dream life!

Do Something

Activity Prompt

Time for Accountability!

1. Take a picture of your completed treasure map and post it in the group!

2. What 3 things are you committed to this week to help you reach your first landmark? Post it in the group!

STOP! Have you completed all the action steps in this section? Double check before continuing...

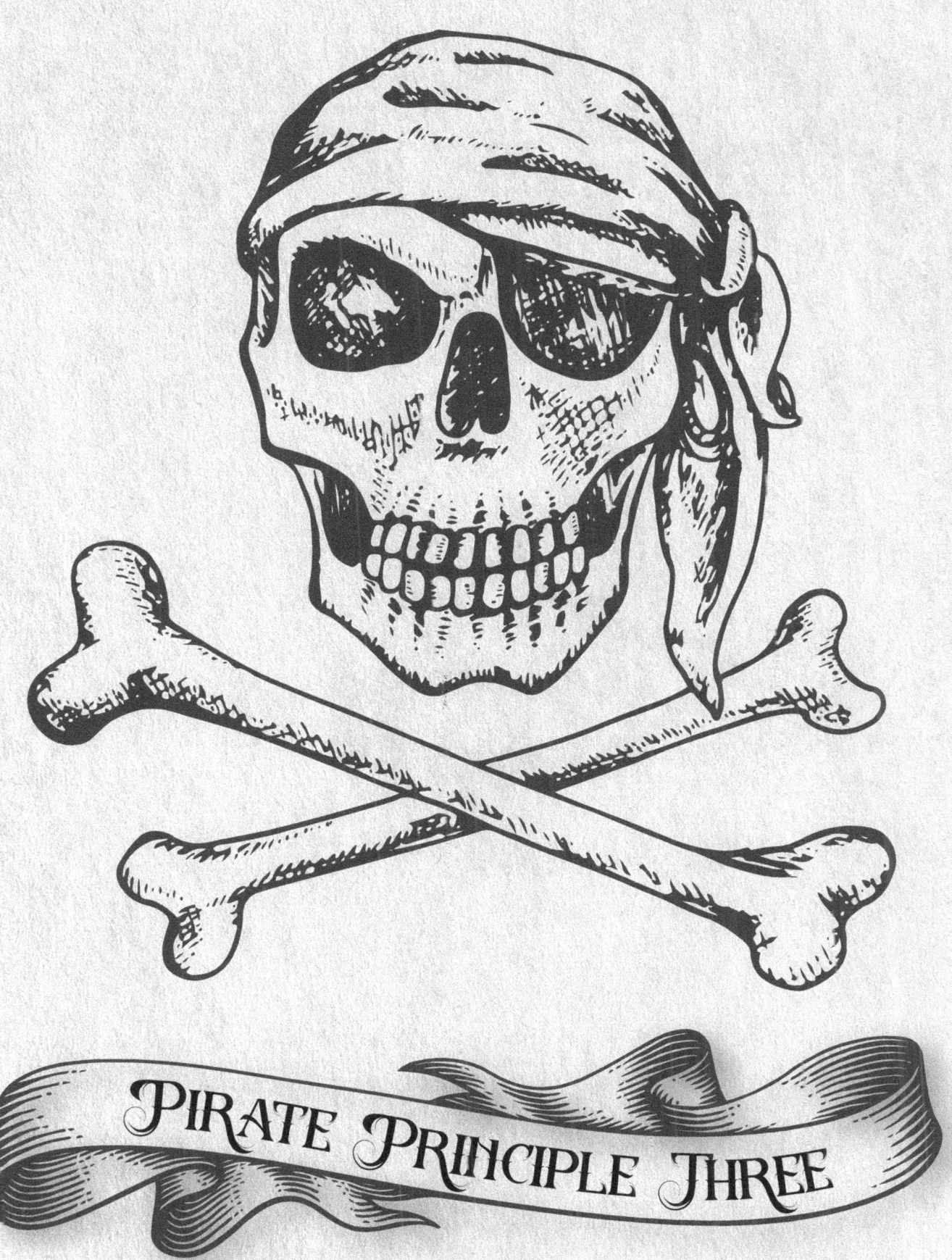

PIRATE PRINCIPLE THREE

PIRATE PRINCIPLE THREE

Using Blackbeard's Spyglass

The thing about making a plan is that we cannot predict the future. We cannot know exactly what challenges we will face or what opportunities we will be presented with. While goals, plans, maps, all of these things are important it is also important to keep ourselves on track AND recognize when we are off course.

Ship captains do this by plotting courses, reading maps, using compasses and using the tools set up for their benefit like buoys and lighthouses. They use tools created for them, we get to create our own.

We have already talked about creating maps and we will continue that throughout the course but I want to pivot slightly to another very important topic - staying on course and doing so without sacrifice.

BUILDING YOUR LIGHTHOUSES

Responsibility, Accountability & Setting Boundaries

The most important piece in all of this is recognizing that the goal is to set up guiding lights, not rigid rules. The idea is to illuminate the path we are on but you don't have to cut off every other path to do so.

Today we are going to talk about Personal Responsibility, Accountability and Setting Boundaries.

We are going to start with boundaries, or as I will refer to them in this course, your Lighthouses.

Imagine if you will that you are on your journey, you know where you are going, your dream life awaits you on Prosperity Isle.

You also know where you need to start, you know what you need to feel stable and be able to make the best decisions based in desire and happiness instead of fear... but things are going to get in your way.

Every once in awhile you are going to find yourself navigating in the dark, dangerously close to the cliffs. If you had to guess, based on your current habits, how did you end up here?

Figuring out the things that disrupt our course and establishing lighthouses to send us a beacon of light as a reminder is key.

Here are some of mine, some I use now, some I have used in the past...

Danger Zone:	Lighthouse:
Blowing my budget on Amazon.	Everything must stay in the cart for 24 hours.
Gas Station Stops / Food Stops when I am showing	Pack food - not just healthy stuff either. Pack a combination of things as well as drinks so I am not tempted to get something else.
Going overboard on gifts for holidays	Plan out my shopping and decide exactly what I am buying for everyone before buying anything and stick to the list.
Blowing the budget on random travel and fun stuff	Create a separate savings for this so I never have to say no if I don't want to.

ACTIVITY PROMPT

List as many of these danger zones you can think of as well as a solution. I have also used questions as my lighthouse, things like:

Do I really want this?
Do I want this more than I want <insert current goal>?
Does this get me closer or further away to my dream life?
Am I doing this because I want to or because I feel like I have to?

Your lighthouses only need to matter and make sense to you. They are there to remind you and help you stay on course.

Another great way to identify other danger zones is to go back to those money beliefs you wrote out. What behaviors have they created that may hold you back or create resistance? What other feelings do you have that create resistance? What is that resistance really about?

I realized that I struggled to stick to a budget because I felt controlled by it. I felt stifled and if I am honest with myself I have felt that way most of my life. I never felt like my uniqueness was appreciated and while they don't seem related they are! A strict budget makes me feel the same way.

Once I realized that was the issue, 1. I couldn't unknow it. 2. I could logically walk myself through.

There is no reason to rebel against myself. These aren't really even rules, these are guidelines, more so they are the steps I have decided I WANT to take to get to my goals. I can change them any time they don't feel aligned. This is actually the best way for me to have control of the future I want.

STOP! Go to the reflection pages at the back of this book to take action and complete this activity prompt!

GIVE YOURSELF THE BOOTY

Do not hold out on yourself.
Allow yourself to enjoy the journey.

Create a reward system for yourself that you are excited about! Don't make yourself earn all the fun things in life, just add extra perks as you get closer to your goals!

A fun example of this is booking a vacation several months out and every time you have an achievement you get to book another piece of the trip.

For example, the date of the trip could reflect how long you think it will take to reach the first stop on your dream life. You could add this trip as an additional savings category on the budget. As you take each action and achieve each thing, you pay for the next piece. When you reach your goal everything is set and waiting for you!

Other examples are upgrading equipment or buying new equipment for a hobby, going out to a really expensive place you have been wanting to go to, planning an extra special date night every few weeks etc. Just like the lighthouses, these are there just for you! This reward is there to positively reinforce yourself as you strive towards your goals. Don't forget, you have to spend money on your rewards and your rewards need to be for you! It doesn't work if you reward yourself by giving your reward to your kids! Also, if you have a partner doing this with you at least some of the rewards should be separate.

PERSONAL RESPONSIBILITY

Everything that has happened up until now, is the result of the choices we made along the way.

When it comes to staying on track, reaching our goals and really claiming the life we desire it is important to remember that everything that has happened up until now, everything and person in our lives right now is the result of some choice we made along the way - yes the exceptional, the good, the bad, the ugly and the mundane.

This isn't always a fun thing to think about and sometimes it down right sucks. Many of these choices may not have felt like choices and there may even be things we wish never happened...

BUT... taking responsibility doesn't create blame, it doesn't lay fault, it simply brings awareness that we can choose something differently this time, next time and any other time.

When we recognize that we have the power of choice, sacrifice disappears. Is it really sacrifice when you choose the thing you would rather have?

This doesn't mean you will always choose vacation, remember those things you need to feel financially secure? If those things are what you really value, you will naturally choose them first. The key is knowing when you do it because you WANT to, not because you feel like you have to.

Would you choose to be homeless so you could travel more? Probably not, but some people would. No answer is right or wrong, it is about what brings you joy and choosing it every time.

Do Something

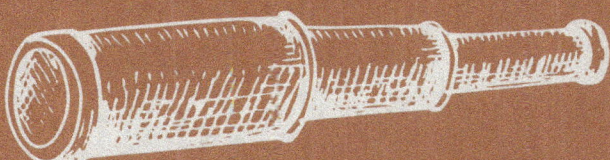

Activity Prompt

Time for Accountability!

What are your 3 action steps for this week?

Use the reflection pages at the back of this workbook to complete this activity prompt before moving on in the workbook.

STOP! Have you completed all the action steps in this section? Double check before continuing...

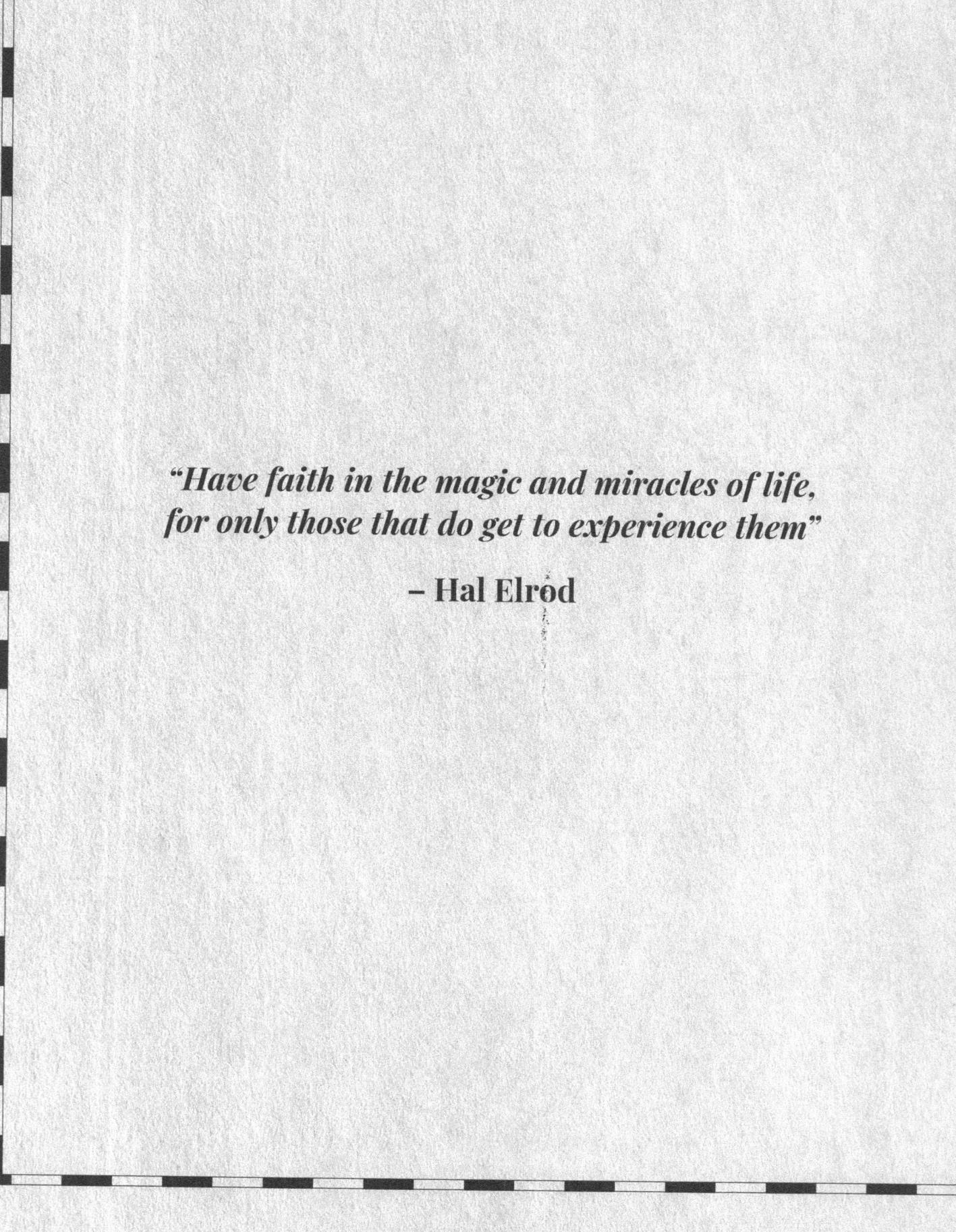

*"Have faith in the magic and miracles of life,
for only those that do get to experience them"*

– Hal Elrod

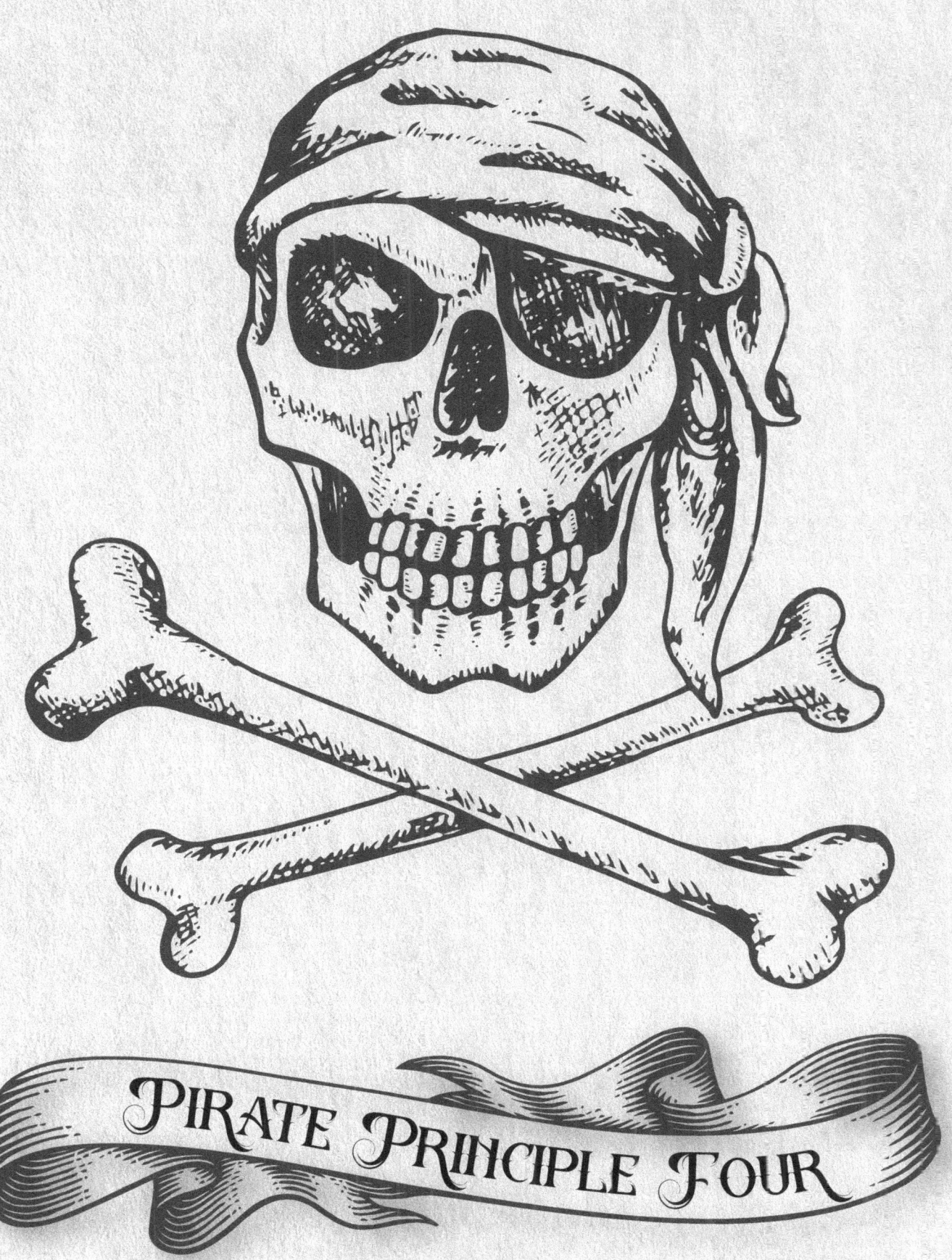

PIRATE PRINCIPLE FOUR

PIRATE PRINCIPLE FOUR

Make Shame and Guilt Walk the Plank

Shame and guilt are common themes in life, especially surrounding money and especially for younger generations. Wanting to build and live a life that goes against the grain, seek balance and joy while working to build wealth is a new concept and one that doesn't always have the best reputation.

Living for a paycheck, working 40 years for a pension just to retire when you are too old to enjoy it, remaining over financed or not financed at all - these are principles of the past that perpetuate feelings of guilt and shame around the way we choose to live.

Today, we are going to break apart these feelings once and for all and create a new path and a map to keep us on track.

DEFINING SHAME AND GUILT

Step 1 - Write out what Shame and Guilt mean to you when it comes to money:

Use at least one example of when you have felt these feelings about your choices, circumstances or journey. If you are struggling with this, think of a time that you denied yourself something you really wanted or felt like you didn't deserve what you have.

Really go deep, take your time and find the root of this feeling. Maybe it is tied back to a memory, maybe a belief you or someone you respect holds true.

Shame:

_____
_____
_____
_____
_____
_____

Guilt:

_____
_____
_____
_____
_____
_____

"Shame is a focus on self, Guilt is a focus on behavior...
Shame is I am bad - Guilt is I did something bad.
Guilt is I made a mistake - Shame is I AM a mistake."

- Brene' Brown

STOP! Make sure to complete this exercise before moving forward. Need more space? Use the reflection pages at the back of this workbook!

Step 2 – Break them down one at a time:

a) Shame:

Shame is really about deservedness. Do we deserve what we have, do we deserve the things we desire? Are we good enough to have these things, do these things and live the life we dream about…

Going back to what we have learned so far -

Example:
I should be further along financially, things have never been that hard…

Ask questions and walk ourselves logically through the answers - with one key difference. Answer as if your best friend is asking you the question about them.

Am I deserving of an amazing life?

Am I deserving of everything I have ever wanted?

Does the fact that some people have had it harder than me invalidate the challenges I have faced?

Does the fact that some people have had it harder than me change the fact that I am where I am because of my choices?

Should I be proud of the life I have built for myself?

Is it ok to want more and still be proud of how far I have come?

STOP! Go to the reflection pages at the back of this book to take action and complete this activity prompt!

ACTIVITY PROMPT

Create a Treasure Trail to Map ourselves out! Follow the Treasure Trail:

Example:
I should be further along financially, things have never been that hard...

Use the prompts below to map out your own treasure trail...

Landmark 1: Overarching Question - Is this really true? Examples of questions to ask to find out: How can I be more proud of where I am? What are some examples of where I made really good choices that allowed parts of my life to be easier? What is an example of when I have overcome adversity?

Landmark 2: Overarching Question - Why do I want to feel this way? Examples of questions to ask to find out: Why do I want things to be hard? Why do I think I need to be further? What does further even mean? What do I get out of making myself suffer with these thoughts?

Landmark 3: How do I want to feel instead? Examples of questions to ask to find out: What feelings motivate me to reach for my goals?

i.e.: Empowered. I want to feel empowered by the choices I have made up until now instead of shameful..

Landmark 4: Is my New Belief Logical? Examples of questions to ask to find out: Is feeling empowered logical? What does it mean to feel empowered? When was the last time I felt empowered? How can I feel empowered now?

Landmark 5: How can I believe this even more? This is a great time to meditate and talk to your higher self!

Landmark 6: What Actions Can I Take RIGHT NOW to reinforce this belief? List at least 3!

STOP! Make sure to complete this activity on the next 2 pages before moving on in the workbook! If you need more space - use the reflection pages in the back of this workbook.

THE DREAM LIFE TREASURE TRAIL CONTINUES

START

Describe a feeling of shame you have about money in a single statement:

_____
_____
_____
_____

Landmark #1:

_____
_____
_____
_____
_____

Landmark #2:

_____
_____
_____
_____
_____

Landmark #3:

_____
_____
_____
_____
_____

Landmark #4:

Landmark #5:

Landmark #6:

X MARKS THE SPOT

Your X is the 1 thing you picked from your dream life!

b) Guilt:

Guilt is a whole different animal than shame but they are both about letting go.

Where shame is really about deservedness, guilt is about expectations - mostly those of other people.

There is value in feelings of remorse when we wrong others but that isn't the same as having unending feelings of guilt, feelings of always letting people down, feelings of being undeserving of the life you have built.

This toxic guilt comes from external pressures and expectations, it comes from perfectionism and overall it comes from lack of self worth.

We all suffer from guilt to varying degrees. Another great measure of these feelings is, how often do you push your accomplishments off as lucky or no big deal? How well do you receive compliments?

If you find yourself being unable to receive praise or own the amazing things you have created in life, this likely comes from feelings of guilt and sometimes shame also.

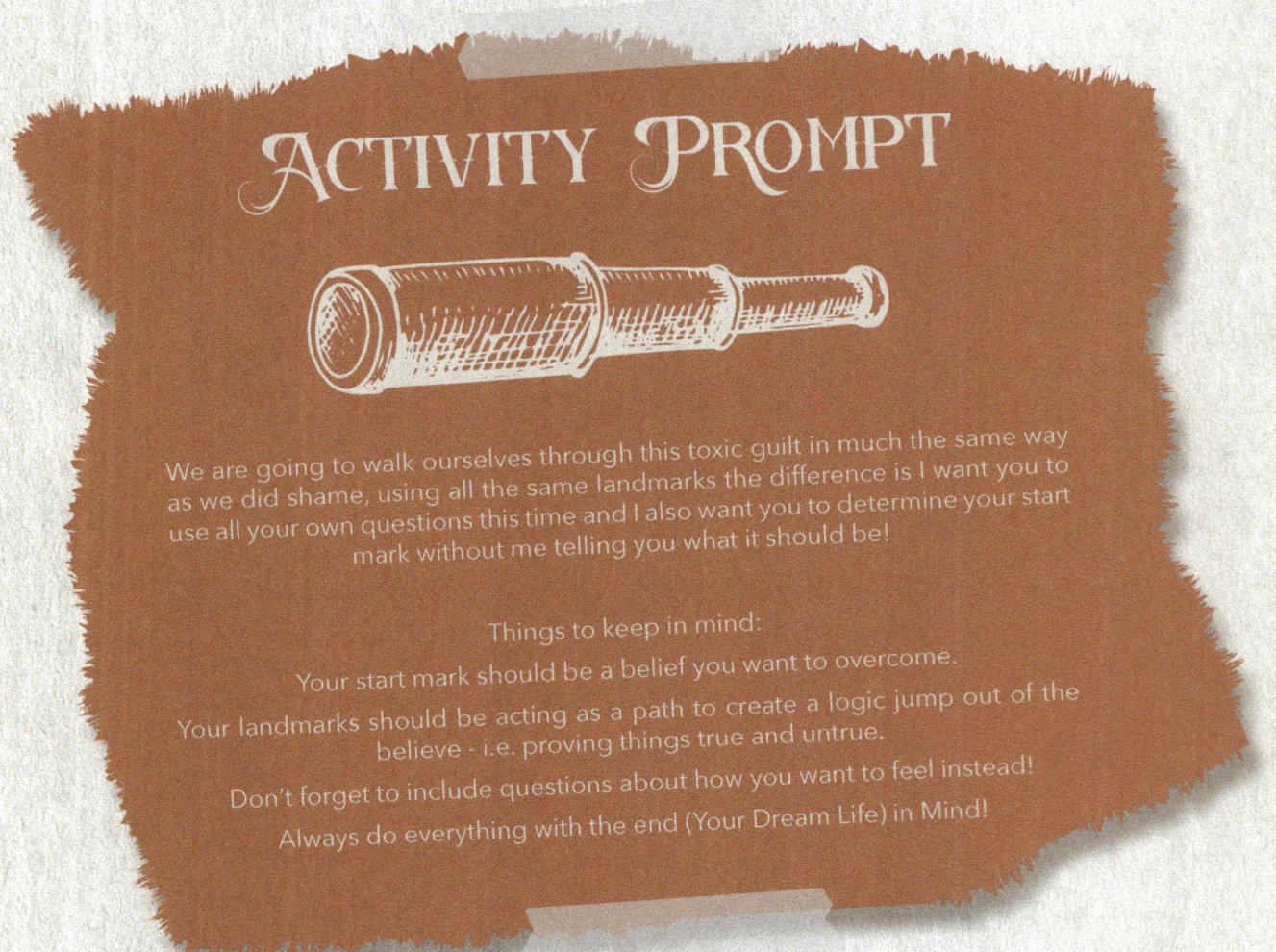

ACTIVITY PROMPT

We are going to walk ourselves through this toxic guilt in much the same way as we did shame, using all the same landmarks the difference is I want you to use all your own questions this time and I also want you to determine your start mark without me telling you what it should be!

Things to keep in mind:

Your start mark should be a belief you want to overcome.

Your landmarks should be acting as a path to create a logic jump out of the believe - i.e. proving things true and untrue.

Don't forget to include questions about how you want to feel instead!

Always do everything with the end (Your Dream Life) in Mind!

Pirate Hack:

Keep all your questions! You can reuse them in future maps. Don't be afraid to dig deep into this, the deeper you go the more the shift will propel you forward, as we move into the money management piece of this course, the more clarity you have the better!

STOP! Make sure to complete this activity on the next 2 pages before moving on in the workbook! If you need more space - use the reflection pages in the back of this workbook.

THE DREAM LIFE TREASURE TRAIL CONTINUES

START

Landmark #1:

Landmark #2:

Landmark #3:

Landmark #4:

_____
_____
_____
_____
_____
_____

Landmark #5:

_____
_____
_____
_____
_____
_____
_____

Landmark #6:

_____
_____
_____
_____
_____
_____
_____
_____

X MARKS THE SPOT

Your X is the 1 thing you picked from your dream life!

_____
_____
_____
_____
_____
_____
_____

Do Something

Activity Prompt

Write 3 affirmations based on your discoveries. Put them somewhere easy to reach and say them outloud to yourself every morning and every evening.

Example: I have created all the wonderful things in my life and am deserving of everything I desire!

AVAST

STOP! Have you completed all the action steps in this section? Double check before continuing...

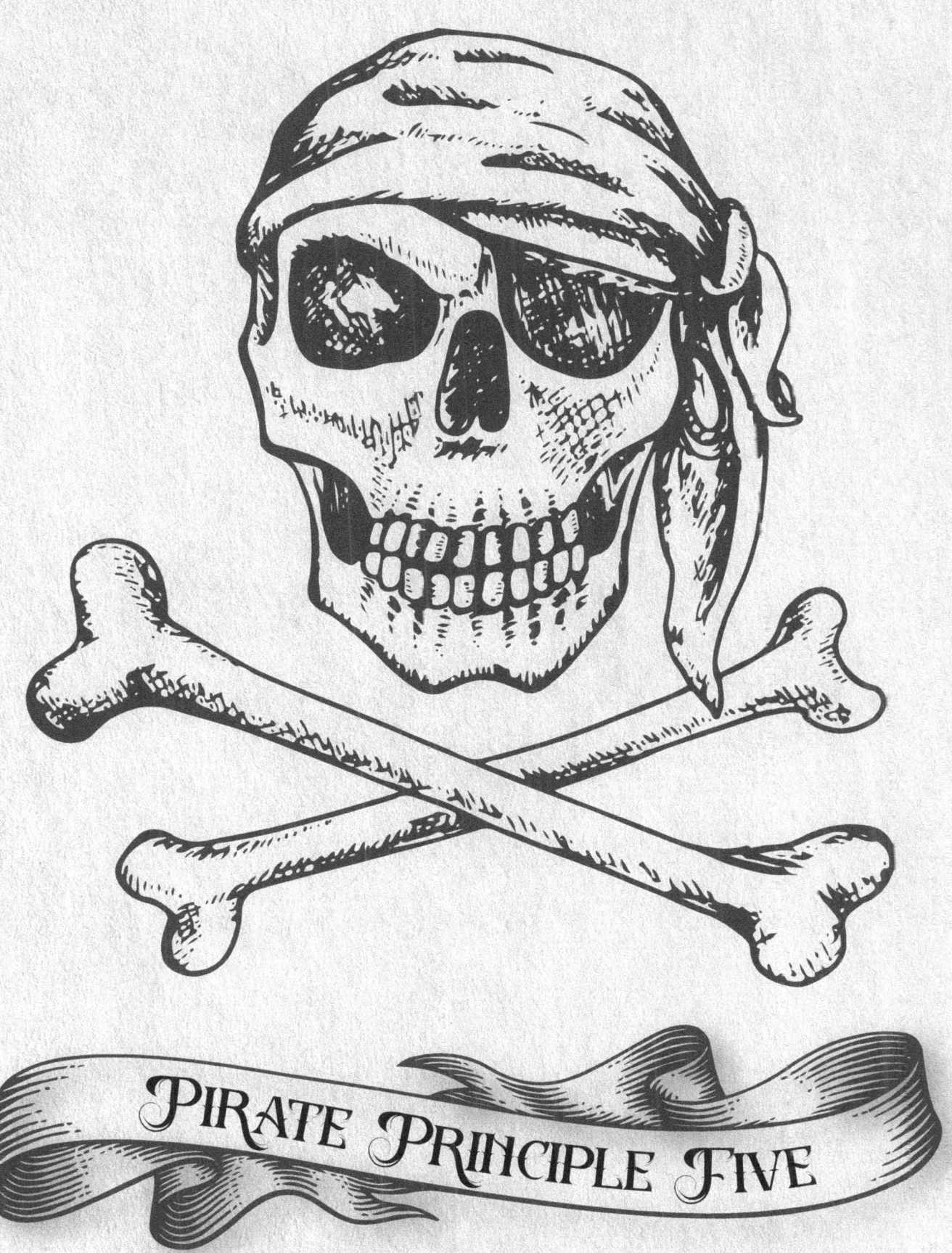

PIRATE PRINCIPLE FIVE

PIRATE PRINCIPLE FIVE

Build a Treasure Chest for Your Gold

It is important to learn how to protect your money and your ability to live in alignment without falling back into scarcity. The best way to do that is through the development of tools and resources!

Just like a treasure chest protects the rich stuff of pirates, your bank of tools and resources will protect your treasure - not just your money either!

Tools and Resources

Tools: Things you use to keep you on track towards your goals, even your goals are tools! This also incluces things like your budget, a spending plan, your lighthouses etc.

Resources: Are cash, things you can turn into cash, things you can use to find more cash (like cash flow planning), sources of income, excellent credit, available credit, investments, property equity etc.

It is important to have both tools and resources, the key to financial independence is your ability to adjust and be resourceful when an issue arises or you are presented with an opportunity. The tools help keep you on track, find and build your resources and your resources give you options.

Activity Prompt

Using the reflection pages at the back of this workbook, answer the following questions:

What Tools and Resources Do You Currently have?
What Tools and Resources do You want to have?
What is the one tool and one resource you could create today that would make everything else easier?

STOP! Go to the reflection pages at the back of this book to take action and complete this activity prompt!

TEMPLATES LIBRARY

On page 61 you will find a templates library featuring my 5 signature financial tools. Use these as-is or as inspiration to create your own tools.

ACTIVITY PROMPT

Use the templates provided to create your own tools for 1-6. Create the tool from part 1 as well. Create the Resource from Part 1 or 3 action steps to get you there.

Note: In the training session we will focus on creating categories for the budget based on everything they have done so far and talking about the spending plan, budget and minimum spending requirements. This will include spending, saving and investing categories.

In the crows nest call we will go over the financial audit, minimum spending, the values worksheet and talk about the one they created.

I will officially release access to the couples course and encourage a 1:1 call for the financial audit.

AVAST

STOP! Have you completed all the action steps in this section? Double check before continuing...

PIRATE PRINCIPLE SIX

PIRATE PRINCIPLE SIX

The Pirate's Life is the Life for Me!

Committing to aligning all the pieces of your life both with your values and financially can be a bit overwhelming. As we go through this process, I encourage you to give yourself grace, focus on short term goals and revisit this section often. Feel free to reference earlier modules for help.

Pirate Hack - If you feel like you need it do not be afraid to create a tool or a resource to provide more support in an area you struggle with, for example, hiring a personal trainer or taking career advancing classes.

STEP INTO ALIGNMENT

ACTIVITY PROMPT

We have spoken about the 8 areas of alignment in Pirate Principle Two, but now it is time to really get into it! In each area you are going to do the following:

Create a goal that costs money that you will accomplish in no more than 90 days. Don't make this goal too big, think step 1 of something larger - it has to cost money though.

Write out which value it reflects.

Identify which step in your dream life map it is connected to.

Assign a reward for when you accomplish it - the reward also needs to cost money

Write out at least 1 Danger Zone / Lighthouse for each goal

Make a list of any tool or resource you will use to reach the goal

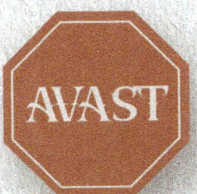

AVAST

STOP! Have you completed all the action steps in this section? Double check before continuing...

Note: During the session we will be talking about the importance of spending in this process to reinforce the alignment We will also be talking about the importance of small goals and goals that tie in multiple areas. I will create my own map to use as an example.

"Do not stop thinking of life as an adventure. You have no security unless you can live bravely, excitingly, imaginatively; unless you can choose a challenge instead of competence."

– Eleanor Roosevelt

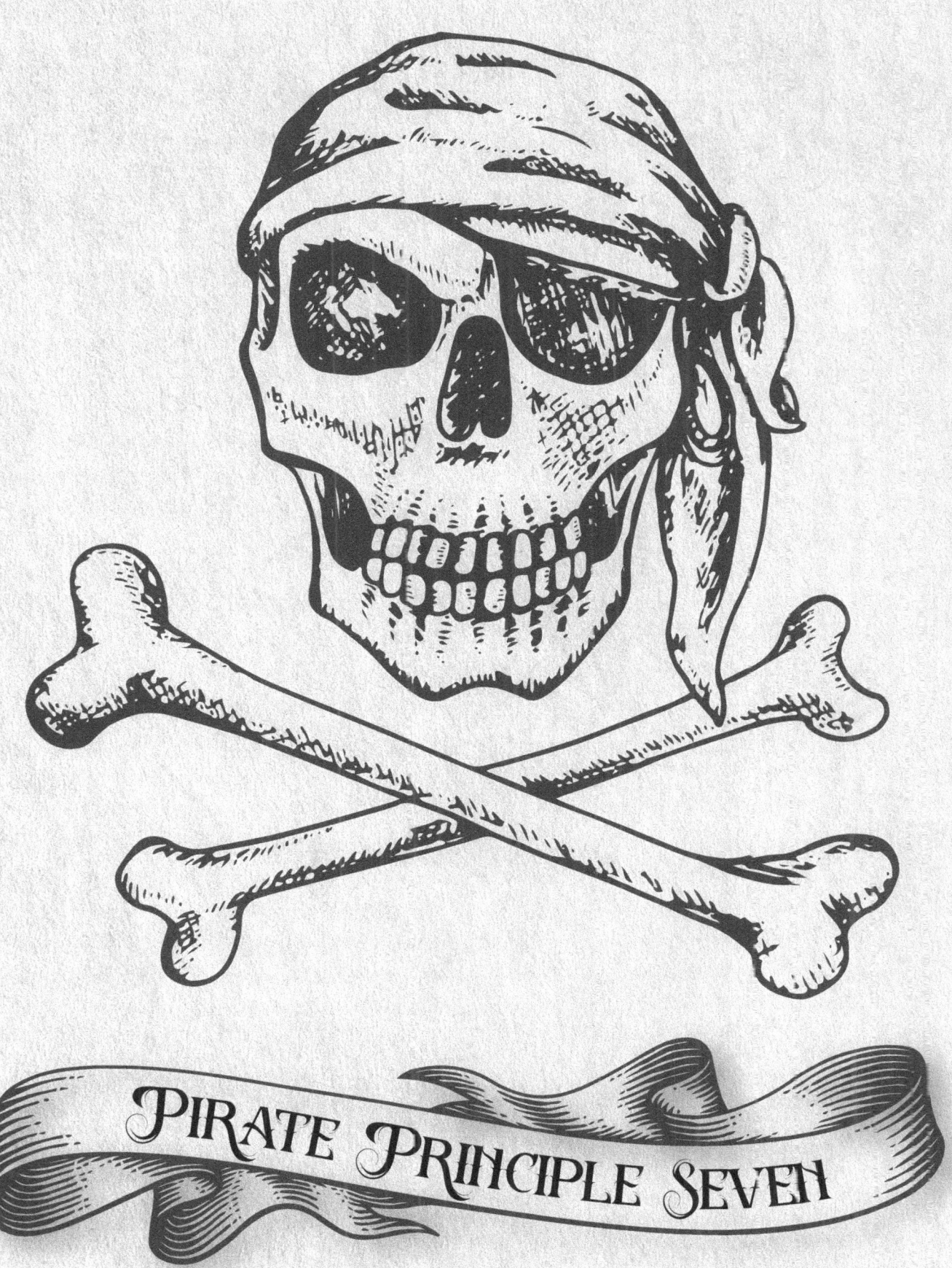

PIRATE PRINCIPLE SEVEN

PIRATE PRINCIPLE SEVEN

How to Split the Booty

It is time to talk about aligned decision making! All that work you just did diving into the 8 areas of alignment is going to come in handy as you put all the mapping skills you have learned to the test!

How you make financial decisions in the moment is the true test of all that we have done in this course. It can be tough to say no to things that no longer fit but it can be just as difficult to give yourself permission to say yes.

As we break down decision making you will be both mapping to the decision AND squashing those pesky limiting beliefs as we go. As soon as one comes up, pause and start asking - "is that really true?" Learning how to coach yourself through and prove or disprove things using logic will make decision making infinitely easier.

MAPPING THE DECISION

Start: Buying Decision

Landmark 1: What Category of Alignment does this fall in? Does it get you closer or further away from your end goal?

Landmark 2: What Value Does it Support? Is it a top 5 Value? How does prioritizing spending money on this value ahead of others make you feel?

Landmark 3: Does it take away from a higher ranking goal? Is this the best way to serve this value?

Landmark 4: What priority number is it (1-4)? If it is a number 4 (Everything Else) - On a scale of 1-10 how much joy will it bring? Will it contribute to your income earning ability later?

Landmark 5: Why do you want it? Do you want it more than (pick something else that relates to a different goal)?

Landmark 6: When I think of the overall picture of my dream life, how does this fit?

X Marks the Spot: Is this in alignment? If you decide NO, ask yourself one more question, why?

The reason is, this will help you to determine if this is a no, a not yet or a no that should be a yes but you are making it from fear.

I want you to do this first round of questions not based on if you can afford it, remember it is about if it is in ALIGNMENT. A yes can absolutely be a not yet while you work on finding or creating the resources. A hard NO cancels manifestation, we only want to use that if it is not in alignment.

Pirate Hack: Never ask yourself if you deserve something or if something is "worth it". Your questions need to stay focused on if it is alignment and moves you closer or further from your goals

ACTIVITY PROMPT

Create your treasure map using the landmarks and prompts above!

THE DREAM LIFE TREASURE TRAIL CONTINUES

Buying Decision:

START

_____
_____
_____
_____

Landmark #1:

_____
_____
_____
_____
_____

Landmark #2:

_____
_____
_____
_____
_____
_____

Landmark #3:

_____
_____
_____
_____
_____

Landmark #4:

Landmark #5:

Landmark #6:

X MARKS THE SPOT

Your X is the 1 thing you picked from your dream life!

"A goal is just a dream with a deadline."

-- Napoleon Holl

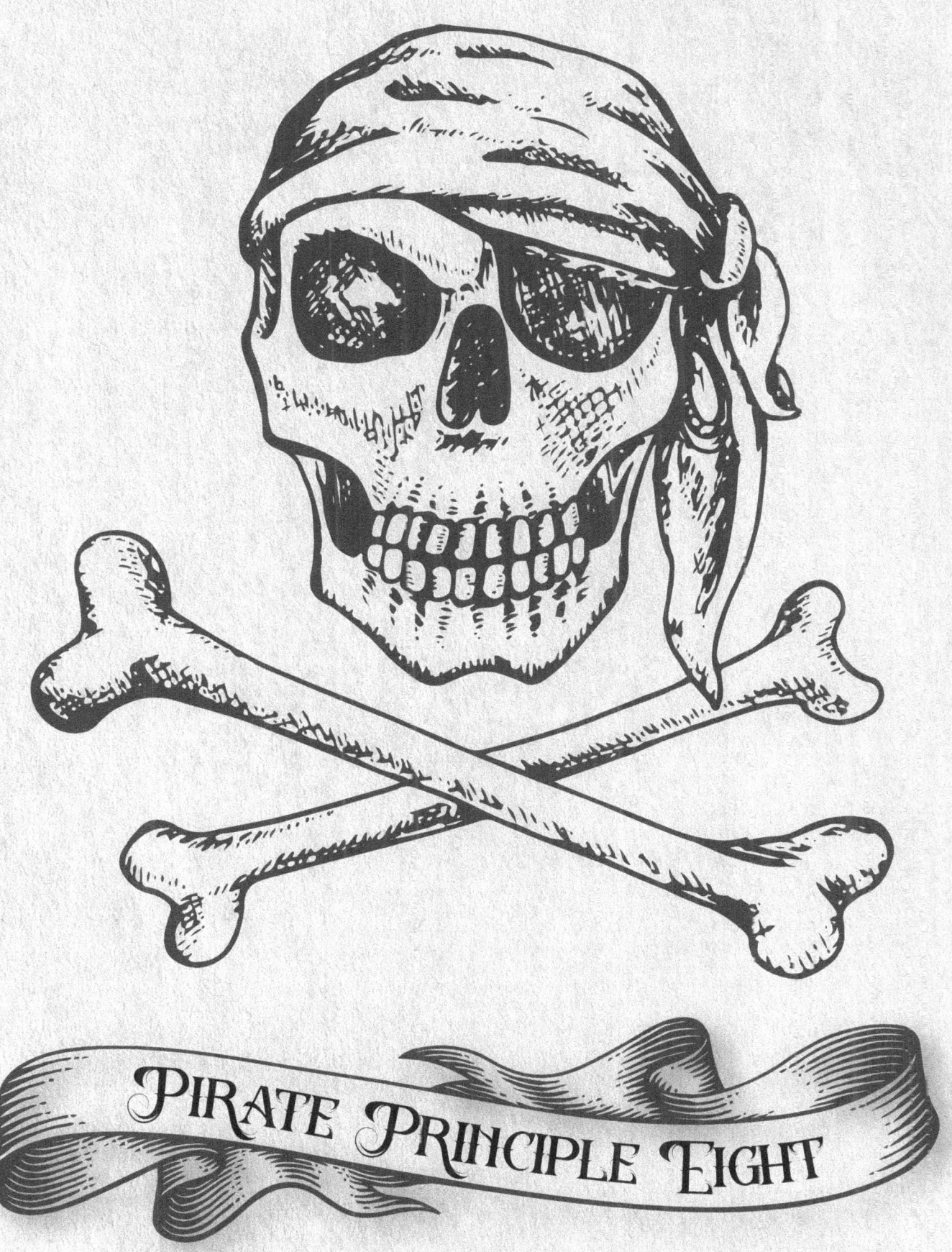

PIRATE PRINCIPLE EIGHT

PIRATE PRINCIPLE EIGHT

The Obligations of a Pirate Cartographer

You have done it! You have reached prosperity isle and now it is time to decide how you want to build your wealth! This is where we will be breaking down ways to build wealth and comparing them with your dream life to once again decide if it is in alignment.

I am not a licensed financial advisor, I will not be making recommendations for investment. The purpose of this module is to help you understand the importance of diversifying your investments, creating multiple sources of income and doing so in a way that still allows you to live the lifestyle you want. For example, don't start a business that requires you to work nights and weekends if you want to spend that time doing something else! Don't invest in high risk things if you are not comfortable with it etc.

Money Making Map

There are millions of ways to make money in this world, for the purposes of this final map you will be choosing, you guessed it - 6!

We will be separating the wealth building into categories to start but keep in mind there could be many options left out, this is meant to be an overview but opportunities reach as far as your imagination does!

You don't need something from every category, but I encourage you to have 3 categories.

Not on this list but also part of the conversation is cash / savings - anything 100% liquid.

Entrepreneurship/ Sources of Income	Assets - Property and Collectables	Insurance	Stocks/ Bonds/ Funds/ Annuities	Pensions/ 401k/ Self Funded Pensions

Here is a sample treasure map (this is mine and I did more than 6 landmarks).

Landmark 1: Non-passive sources of income. i.e. Real Estate Sales, Property Management, Fempreneur Events, Financial Coaching, Credit Repair, The Pirate Pack, Retreats, Aarons Career/ Salary and Bonuses.

Landmark 2: Passive sources of income. i.e.10 Rental Properties (I go back and forth but i may look for an apartment building instead of single units). Short Term Rentals - Several (Goal 8) rentals on single property in Northern Alaska Self Storage

Landmark 3: Assets. 7 Figure Equity between personal properties - Not income

Landmark 4: Assets. 7 Figure Equity in income properties.

Landmark 5: Life insurance. $1 million on each of us.

Landmark 6: Stocks/ Bond/ Funds. 500k in traditional investments.

Landmark 7: Liquid. $30k in sacred savings mutual fund, $10k in budget balancing fund, $10k in emergency fund, $50k in opportunity fund.

Landmark 8: 401k, Aaron's 401k.

Landmark 9: Other (could go under stocks but I like to keep this separate), Aaron's company shares.

X Marks the Spot

Each one of these things allow me to embrace my life of freedom. Full transparency is my 10 year plan to retirement, we are still working on pretty much every category. We have also bought and sold properties, had rentals, done flips and other things as we have decided what we liked and did not like. This is not set in stone, it should be fluid, it builds on itself and it always leads to the dream life of alignment you designed!

Do Something

Activity Prompt

Create your money making map using the next two pages. Consider the categories listed earlier in this chapter, and categories that are not listed.

Remember: X Marks the spot of your dream life!

AVAST

STOP! Make sure to complete this activity on the next 2 pages before moving on in the workbook! If you need more space - use the reflection pages in the back of this workbook.

"I don't have to chase extraordinary moments of happiness - it's right in front of me if I am paying attention and practicing gratitude."

-- Brene' Brown

THE DREAM LIFE TREASURE TRAIL CONTINUES

START

Landmark #1:

Landmark #2:

Landmark #3:

Landmark #4:

_____
_____
_____
_____
_____
_____

Landmark #5:

_____
_____
_____
_____
_____

Landmark #6:

_____
_____
_____
_____
_____
_____
_____

X MARKS THE SPOT

Your X is the 1 thing you picked from your dream life!

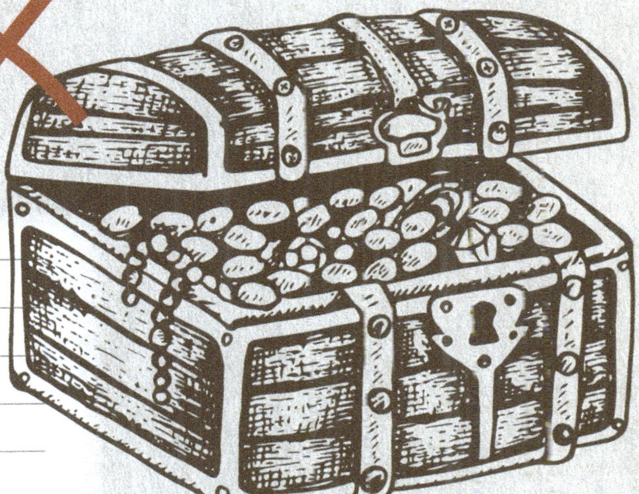

_____
_____
_____
_____
_____
_____
_____

"I've learned that making a 'living' is not the same as 'making a life."

– Maya Angelou

THE TEMPLATE LIBRARY

Breaking Down the Elements of a Spending Plan

Personal Spending Audit and Identifying Financial Priorities

Step 1: Break your bank account into specific categories and categorize everything!

This should include every account where you spend money, all credit cards, all bank accounts etc.

The categories should be specific. Try to break down stores like walmart into household goods, food, clothing etc.

Don't forget to look at your online order history to create categories.

This will be an ongoing, fluid document as you get to know your habits on a deeper level so do your best at the beginning but give yourself room to break things down even further.

Step 2: Prioritize Every Transaction

Just like categorizing everything is important, understanding how every transaction, purchase, decision to save etc. impacts your life is also important.

Step 3: Evaluate and decide if you are happy with the way spent your money in the last 90 days.

It is okay if you are, it is okay if you regret NOT buying something, it is also okay if you are not 100% sure.

It is really important to be as honest with yourself as you can during the process. Think about where you are going, is there anything you could have done, that you wish you would have done that would bring you closer?

Really look at anything that you consider an impulse decision. Did it bring you joy? If you had waited 24 hours would you still have bought it or done it?

Make a comprehensive list of what you would have changed and assign a dollar value and balance the amounts. This amount will become part of the budget.

Building a Spending Plan & Budget

To break the paycheck to paycheck cycle, you must first have goals and understand deeply what you want, this is a Spending Plan. A budget is then the nitty gritty details of how you will execute your spending plan. Both are necessary to build TRU Financial Stability.

Elements of a Spending Plan

Spending Audit

A complete breakdown of how you have spent your money over the last 90 days including specific categories and noting any changes you would make.

Financial Priorities Audit

All of your spending separated into priorities 1-4 based on the TRU Prosperity Priorities worksheet.

Specific Goals with Timelines

At least 3 long term goals with smaller goals that create a path to success is necessary. Make sure you think long term and short term.

Elements of a Budget

All Income for the Full 14month Period

Don't forget to include potential bonuses, tax returns or any other potential income you will likely get.

All of the Spending Audit Categories

It is imperative that your budget be as specific as possible. It may seem daunting at first, but the more specific your budget categories are the easier it will be to reach your goals.

Savings and Goal Categories

You should have savings and goal categories that are specific just like spending categories.

Create Specific Goals with Timelines and Dollar Amounts

Step 1: Create ALL the financial goals you want to accomplish in the next 12-14 months.

Start with the big picture of what you want to create and work backwards.

Every goal should include a timeline, list of tasks and have dollar amounts associated with each step.

Categorize every goal as appropriate, some will have their own categories but adding to savings, paying off debt etc. may fall under one of your spending categories.

Make your goals specific. Keep asking - "How do I do that?" and then write out a task list. Repeat the exercise until you have a complete list of every single thing you need to accomplish and a dollar amount associated with completing all of your goals.

Breaking Down the Elements of a Spending Plan & Budget

Income, Bonuses, Tax Returns, Settlements, Side Gigs...

How do you decide what goes in your budget and what should just be extra?

Simple - It ALL goes in the budget. I know this can seem scary, what if it is less, what if it doesn't come through, these fears often keep people from budgeting with all of their resources.

Reasons to use it all:

If you don't you will waste the money. It will inevitably become slush fund money, celebration money or victim to some other NOT well thought out plan.

Just because you include it in your budget doesn't mean you include inconsistent amounts in your priority 1, 2 or even 3 categories. Remember, everything goes in the budget including goals, savings, vacations etc.

In order to be effective and intentional with your money, it has to be ALL of your money. We make better financial decisions when we don't make them in the moment.

How do you make sure you get ALL of your expenses into your budget, even the ones you don't know about?

Step 1: Look to your Spending Audit and add all your categories.

Step 2: Analyze Everything

Analyze everything that has "stolen your savings" in the last year and rate it 1-3 on the likelihood if it happening again.

1 - Not Likely: Don't worry about it.

2 - Unsure: Add the total to your savings goals

3 - Likely: Add it your the budget as its own category

Step 3: Plan for ALL Holidays and Special Occasions

Make a list of every holiday, special occasion, birthday etc. that you like to celebrate. Assign a dollar amount to it and add it to your budget. The "due date" should be 2 weeks before the event to make sure you have the money in time.

How do you create a Budget that Serves you, Breaks the Paycheck to Paycheck Cycle and creates financial stability?

Create a budget that includes goals that create the stability you crave and build the life you want.

Step 1: Transfer all of your Goals

Transfer all of your goals from your spending plan into your budget. Don't forget to add in ALL of your savings categories.

Step 2: Balance Your Cash Flow

Make sure that you keep a positive cash flow throughout the year between pay periods. This may require you to adjust your due dates.

Step 3: Everything gets a due date - even grocery shopping.

Step 4: Prioritize your Goals

Prioritize your goals based on what makes you feel stable. Make it clear in your budget which goals get funded first.

Assets

Something you own that has value, Cash and property equity.

Asset Type/Name	$ Amount
Total:	

Liabilities

Debt, financial obligations, items on payment plans, etc.

Liability Type/Name	$ Amount
Total:	

Value of Assets [less/minus] Value of Liabilities = Total Net Worth

IDENTIFYING FINANCIAL PRIORITIES

Survival	$ Amount
Percent of Total Budget:	

Protect Ability to Earn	$ Amount
Percent of Total Budget:	

Current Obligations	$ Amount
Percent of Total Budget:	

Everything Else	$ Amount
Percent of Total Budget:	

SEPARATE YOUR SAVINGS

Identifying where your savings is allocated is just as important as saving your money. It starts with prioritizing and categorizing your savings, the same way you'd prioritize your spending.

Priority	Type of Savings	Current $	Total Goal $

SEPARATE YOUR SAVINGS

I challenge you to embrace the idea of living your life on your own terms and with complete intention. Design your dream life and from that day forward spend 100% of your money making it happen for yourself!

This worksheet will help you identify what is important to you and where your money should be going. You will then grade yourself on how well you are doing spending according to the identified values.

Directions:

Rank the list in each category 1-5 based on importance – remember this is your dream life we are talking about no matter what your current circumstances.

Rank each Category in order of Importance Identify the top 3 things (can come from any list) – do any of them come from the same category? Is that the same category you ranked number 1? Adjust your ranking of importance if necessary.

Grade yourself A, B, or C based on the % of income you spend in your #1 category / top 3 items.

80-100% A, 50-80% B, Below 50% C

Category 1: Time
Saving Time / Convenience
Family Dinners at home
Family Outings
Date Night with your spouse
Hosting Parties /Events

Category 3: Lifestyle
Beauty Services (Hair, nails, beard trims etc)
Exercise / Healthy Lifestyle
Specific Hygiene products
Nice House / Comfy Environment
Travel / Adventure

Category 2: Entertainment
Sports / Activities (Participation by Adults)
Sports / Activities (Participation by Kids)
Hobbies
Travel / Adventure
Going "Out" (Drinks / Dinners etc)

Category 2: Future Planning
Retiring Comfortably
Saving for Children's College
Investing Money
Becoming / Remaining Debt Free
Retiring Early

REFLECTION PAGES